A Swindler's Grace

Adam LeFevre

New Issues Poetry & Prose

A Green Rose Book

New Issues Poetry & Prose
The College of Arts and Sciences
Western Michigan University
Kalamazoo, Michigan 49008

First Edition, 2016.

ISBN: 978-1-936970-34-6 (paperbound)

Library of Congress Cataloging-in-Publication Data:
LeFevre, Adam.
A Swindler's Grace/Adam LeFevre
Library of Congress Control Number: 2014952965

Editor: William Olsen
Managing Editor: Kimberly Kolbe
Layout Editor: McKenzie Lynn Tozan
Assistant Editor: Alyssa Jewell
Art Direction: Nicholas Kuder
Design: Elise Bobian
Production: Paul Sizer
                              The Design Center, Frostic School of Art
                              College of Fine Arts
                              Western Michigan University
Printing: McNaughton & Gunn, Inc.

A Swindler's Grace

Adam LeFevre

New Issues

WESTERN MICHIGAN UNIVERSITY

Also by Adam LeFevre

Everything All At Once
Ghost Light, a chapbook

For my brother Hatch and my sister Prudence, fellow-travelers who know the territory

Contents

Home

Nature loves to hide

—Heraclitus, Fragment 123

Prologue

Attention

—for Carrie

Some walls contain stillness.
Some, wild and clamorous waves.

All music is leased from a wind
which is neither
here nor there.

When a blackbird stops singing,
when leaves begin to tremble,
that means somewhere
an infant has drawn his first breath.
This world responds.

The moon floats across the night like a lily
gently blown across a pond.
Stars reposition themselves,
breathing down each other's necks,
blinking and crowding in to see
through the one available window.

What will that rippling return?
Hard to say.

When I sing I must bend the air carefully
to represent my soul
bowing to the others, offering
the tempest of my silence,
and these first wisps of words,
getting ready
like a safe-cracker blowing on his fingers.

Thanksgiving

Snow, Christmas Morning

The children freeze.
Perfect rigor.
Good soldiers
called to attention.
Plumb as icicles,
eyes front,
zombie stares

then, commence leaning
slowly back
past the point of no return and
fall
like oaks unbowed
fearlessly
into plush cushions
of an all-night snow,

which they plow
spread-eagled on their backs
with scissoring legs and
mother-hugging arms
as if swimming to the horizon
staring up at a slate sky
through the plaintive reach
of leafless trees
to make the shape of an angel.

Meanwhile muted choirs of the real thing
steel themselves
at the cold edge of heaven
all shimmery and shivering,
certain once they commit to it
there'll be no end to the falling.

Faith is grace ungrounded,
appealing to saints and children.
Dreamers too.
Angels are more realistic
which is why they flail and tumble
and fall and fall.

Ice Storm

There could be werewolves!
At this latitude at least
the rain can suffer in the night
such a change and
lock the world inside itself,
make it not the world
but a likeness displayed behind glass
as in a wax museum.

Cut off in mid-sentence
is it not the custom to stare dumbly at the phone
as if some explanation were about to come?
So today all nature is academic.
How gracefully the trees succumb!
How fatal in this dazzling landscape
articulation is.
We have no power.

The lines are down spitting millions
of tiny stars out over the lacquered road,
stars that were messages.
I saw the sun come up this morning.
It just sort of stood there, stammering and confused,
like a man back from the nightshift
who opens his front door and finds
another man, obviously a musician,
stroking his beautiful unconscious wife.

Nocturne with Cows

Each night the dairyman her husband
sinks like a hoof in the muck of his sleeping
and she rises to her work
out over the stiles
lifting her nightgown
above her knees
to wade the undulant pastures where
with a curtsey, the irony of which
does not vex them,
she dismisses the recumbent
Guernseys from the blue spills
of curdling moonlight
that are her responsibility
to gather and bury
by the hour before dawn.

Halftime

October night nesting on the stadium.
The marching band blasts through a medley of moon songs, 4/4 time.
Moon River. Paper Moon.
Out from the ranks this year's appointed maiden spins,
twirling her silver baton.
Racks of artificial little moons
supported by lofty aluminum poles
define the field she dances on.

She's heavy-thighed, not natural to
the splits and pirouettes she halfway does,
stumbling sometimes on the choppy turf.
In this town grace is not divine. It's work.

Her bosom, squeezed in a sequined leotard, heaves for air.
Her brow gleams with little gems of sweat.
She knows what's going wrong and cares,
but has to keep up with the music til the end,
deferring shame like an inheritance.

Bass drum calmly counts the debt.
The unregenerate horns stampede.
She holds a shaky arabesque, hurls herself spread-eagle
through a wobbly cartwheel.
A smile, immense and frozen, never leaves her face.
Her will to cheer remains sublime
to the tittering of the glockenspiel.

They don't ask much in this factory town.
Pity rises from the smokestacks, acknowledged waste.
All they want from their majorette is her presence,
predictable as the moon's.
She must show. Spread her arms. Smile at each degradation.
Bow deeply to the dropped baton.
Stick to it. Graduate.
Raise sensible children with sensible names
like Jason Jr. and Dawn.
Teach them earthly virtues. Bitterness. Gravity.
Daughter into Mother always smiling,
reminding them this is how it goes,
how it is, and how it has to be.

Coeymans

Dogs bark at strangers.
The local talent has
phobic mothers constantly calling,
in the frail hours, our police.

The local talent has
toppled tombstones, scattered beer cans
in the frail hours. Our police
report routinely in the mornings:

toppled tombstones, scattered beer cans
and condoms on the cemetery grass. Men
report routinely in the mornings
to work at the brickyard or the cement plant.

And condoms on the cemetery grass mean
some lucky souls won't be recruited again
to work at the brickyard or the cement plant,
or suffer star fullbacks between their thighs,

some lucky souls won't be recruited again
to be drunk fathers growling *Do what I say*
or suffer! Star fullbacks between their thighs,
their drunk daughters look up at the sky. It's a blessing

to be drunk. Father's growling *Do what I say*
far away now. Far enough away.
Their drunk daughters look up at the sky. It's a blessing.
And the inscrutable stars.

Far away now. Far enough away.
Dogs bark at strangers,
and the inscrutable stars,
phobic mothers constantly calling.

Something Red, 1959

—for my brother

The woods around our house
started popping in November,
distance muffling the salvoes
of deer-hunters, some sober

all free men bearing arms
against a killing week of
factory alarms
and fates too plain to speak of.

Most wouldn't shoot
more than the law approved.
A few, against a doubt,
shot anything that moved.

We were good boys wolfing breakfast,
keen for a Saturday
til Mother's purled request
we stay in the yard to play.

We fell to howl and bellow
til she caved in to despair,
gave us a look of sorrow
and something red to wear.

Dolled up like Bozos we ran
out singing to warn the deer,
the theme from *Superman*
and the jingle for *Black Label* beer.

In the war between Nature and Man
which cause is right? Which pure?
We chose to be partisan
with the fugitive, Nature,

simply because its style,
aimless and oppressed,
secretive, uncivil
suited us best.

Crisscrossing the ridge-run,
weaving through the trees
like a carnival procession
our feral revelries

stopped in a hollow where
heaped by a mossy rill,
still steaming in the air
the guts of a field-dressed kill

froze us in our tracks.
We squinted in the sun
bleeding through the tamaracks.
Our Dionysian

allegiances converted
headfirst to Apollo.
Profounder delight diverted
us in the now sacred hollow.

Stone silent, philosophic,
we admired the butcher's art.
Then each took up a stick
and probed to find the heart.

Though the tenor of our mission
changed to a darker key
our basic condition
was still ecstacy.

We never gave a thought

to the rhythm in our wrists
as we sought the thing we sought
amid the folds and twists

of rhythmless remains.
We weren't afraid of blood
or the god that blood disdains.
Whatever was was good.

In Memory of My Tail

Why do we long to leave the earth by rising?
Old root, did you suggest another way?

We're higher forms now but not clouds yet.
And life without you is still life in your honor.
I drag behind me all I can,
unraveled dreams and *ubi sunts*
limp and larded with unconsciousness,
a trail of forgetfulness
longer than any one life.

Once I could lean out far and without fear
over the pit where darkness gorged
to savor the odor of my own death there,
you behind me, allowing it,
countering each tilt of my voluptuous head.

Now on my back I stare at the ceiling,
fall asleep lunging for a vertical access.
Crumpled poems plummet past windows in my dreams,
a steady snow of little suicides, failed elegies to you,
my lost ballast, my forsaken unthinking
other mind.

Claiborne's House

When you found newspapers from 1890
lining pantry shelves,
and down in the cellar Ball jars of green beans
and carrots put up Sept. 1929,
the old hitchhiker in you gave up on phoenixes,
gave in to his fondness for old wood and old ways
and took up the mortgage, the rot,
no heat, no running water.

The local pig-farmers snigger at your fancy, this farmhouse
you bought, as they say, for a song,
a century old and swooning like the swan at the end of Swan Lake.
You're crazy not to just let it fall
following Nature's strong suggestion
into the West River and start over, as they say,
from square one.

Not you, by God!
Jack up the beams! Salve the walls, the pipes!

When we came to visit at your first wintering out
you entertained us with your house-lists into the future
and a tour of your treasured artifacts of old Vermont,
still wearing their precious cobwebs and dust.

Bless you, friend.
You've been panhandled by History, that cunning drifter.
Without a penny to his name he finds virtue
in what's jettisoned along the road.

Pardon me for grinning like a pig-farmer
that first night after too much wine in place of heat
when I heard groaning upstairs where you sleep.
You and your new romance.
You and your old wood.

Leo's Flood

"Come April now she's tame as Mabel's cat.
Got fancy restaurants now at water's edge.
I'm talking eighty years ago before
The Army Corps of Engineers devised
The spillways, flumes, and culverts that could take
A run-off like the spring of that one was.

Floods were nothing new to her and none
But the dim or desperate built too near.
Up a bit you figured to be safe.
That's where they got the saying *Dove Street high*.
That year she crested out at thirty feet.
All the way to Pine Knob they got doused.

My Aunt Gladys, bless her, liked to tell
How water followed her right up the stairs.
They took her from her rooftop in a skiff.
So quick the rise all she could save was just
Her harmonium and the family Bible.

I was thirteen, and the things I saw!
The first naked woman ever in my life
Was screaming, clinging to a hogshead barrel.
She called to me, the torrent taking her
Toward Devil's Spit. And that was that.
Her eyes still sometimes fix me in a dream.
I saw a baby pig float by hunched in a cradle.
Lord knows where the human baby was.
Trees, wagons, church pews, shanties swept away.
Dead bodies too. I saw more than my share.

Poor folk back then were the kind lived riverside.
So naturally poor folk were hardest hit.
Uncounted coloreds clobbered in that first surge.
Whole families washed right off the earth.

There were comic things though happened too.
A preacher who'd been tupping someone's wife
For years on the sly was caught in the act, *flagrante!*
Pants down, water rising. How Daddy loved that story!

We took a load of people in that year.
Mama said it was the Christian thing to do.
At one time seven children shared my room.
Among them Ida Mae, who became my wife.
Gone now, bless her, to the other side.

Tell you this—no photograph can do
Justice to the deluge I remember.
We found unhappy rattlesnakes in our cellar
Curled up behind the preserves. And when the river
Settled back she left the strangest presents.
I saw a Holstein hanging upside down
Twenty feet up an elm in Market Square
Like some Christmas thing. Lord, the smell!"

The New Thanksgiving

We parley but we no savvy. So
we keep trading our days for their scorn.
And hunger remains on all our dishes poised
to receive anything of their nervy waves.

We engaged a surrogate to always be home,
a mythic gentle savage who'll wait kneeling on the shore
spreading skeins of woven protein
and regular radio signals to welcome the
elsewhere beings *on a molecular level* here.

Having looked out and up all this time,
having looked in and still dreaming
a common ancestor links us materially
even to what is no longer there,

haven't we survived loneliness radiantly enough
to become a perfect host, primed
to give everything to the first beings to arrive?

Perpetual Care

Like the cobalt wake
of a Bible whale
their belief
darkened a slow wedge
between the stanzas of stones.

There were no clocks there
with commanding tusks angled among the sighs,
soft brown apples scattered across the tampered sod.

There was no grammar for leaving.
The lingering rumor of a purpose
was keeping them like a pet
inside the believing.
They would have to go

where it went—
through the limber tenses up
and away like *pi* to the *nth*,
then down again, Newtonian,
to the gouged earth, the tilled plot,

and the vulgarity of their grief.
Then off again, banking and looping like a pestered jet.
Then gravely back. Always back.
"As if," said one "to braid
the precious light into re-usable wreaths."

Cleopatra Experimenting with Poison

It was *her gift to them*,
said her most faithful handmaid Charmian,
that each in turn, her favored slaves,
play the royal part
til the bane be found
that would most perfectly chill
the perfect bosom of their Queen.

For that they were gathered close
in an anteroom of elegant mosaics
waiting to be called.

Were they happy for it?
No.
But they knew it right
that Beauty die more quickly than a thought,
that Beauty's servants moan and retch,
in agonizing preludes to assure
Death come for her in one stroke
like an enfeebled Caesar
leaving her coifed,
unfazed, still
alluring in her
diaphanous gown.

If there were one among them who refused
and, while the rest in sobs and whispers prayed for good passage,
slipped through the slim anteroom window and ran
down to the river to hide in the rushes and cattails til dark
when she could make her way safely to the sea,
whose servant was she then? And now
whose mother of god is she?

Psalm

Tune elsewhere for praise, Lord of the world.
The good thing in its goodness turns
my advocacy into a toady's cant.

How long have I beat the air for names
hoping to impress you, my host?
How many hosannas turned to ice
just to rime my biblical beard?

Therefore as your breath, the wind,
topples the unholy numerals of our century,
let me keep my peace, celebrating
as you and the dead both do
without joy or sorrow,

                         and pray
that my heart, like a cloud or a stone,
will silent be
made good by your propinquity.

Shelf Life

A Piano for Cora

All that's hard to resist about the impenetrable
is the many impossible ways to penetrate it
and that's all.
There's a good saying: *Toes wiggle in secret inside shoes.*
See how it takes effect considerably before the meaning of it.

If you could have anything you wanted you'd still have to choose
something. One onyx earring perhaps. Or an intrigue
like a pink envelope postmarked Coral Gables
slipped furtively into the pages of Deuteronomy.
Because all value is sentimental value really.

Few words after baby's first will be cause for any joy.
But if human expression were just a by-product of the body/mind duality
sex really would be the same as going to church,
and silence much less articulate than it is.

This doesn't prove the existence of God or anything.
My little remarks have the virtue, not of truth,
but respect for some difference.
If you made a list of the things that most hurt you
what would be third on the list,

coming after *myself* and *others*?
That's important to think about.
Because thinking is listening.
The names constantly whispered in the conduits of your wrists,
those are the ones your love goes by.

Calling

My voice disembodies.
It will not stay where I am.

Let it go then make friends with the distance,
and where there was silence let there be

silence again, but different, more peculiar.
For nothing must return exactly.

Should my voice come back in the rabble of the wind
saying "Distance didn't want me,"

I won't claim it.
It can't get inside me again.

Lament of the Future Perfect

I will be like the weather
when the moon is that dark beer color
changing to gun-metal blue
in the boughs of spruce and alder.

I will surround your house
holding hostage your assertions
just beyond the lamplight spilling
smugly from your windows,

I will be the dark getting darker,
a mirror someone painted with tar,
muttering to myself (as weather does),
spreading the rumor of something between us.

You can't deny what's whispered in the siftings of a mid-night snow
or the sighing that appends your own long laughter.
I will have been your lover, unknown,
the one you can't let go.

Humiliation

As a fire in a piano factory
reminds us pianos
are also firewood

this rude flame rising in my face
discredits the perfection of my solitude
installing in its place
a queasy worldliness

If I keep looking at my feet
it is only to make sure
they have not become one with the ground

This passion to disintegrate!
Is it not the very terror of love?

Shell Game. Bait and Switch

Right now someplace
where you think something is—
some clutch, cubicle, or zone—
is empty of it, and it's gone
forever.

                    Morning star
or silver dollar.
Minute hand. Snippet of
schoolboy Latin verse.
Vintage Pez dispenser.
Your daughter's baby teeth.
A still maturing savings bond.
A baseball signed by PeeWee Reese...

Who cares?
        What it is
                means less
                        than the hollowness
                                coming after.

The past before it happens
                        exists,
a vague current of electricity
too sublime for the mind to register
but a knelling in the belly.

The future with a swindler's grace
without pronouncement comes and goes.

If you invest in what you see you'll lose.
Take my advice. Credit shadows.

Socratic Landscape

When, thinking,
I think about the thinking in my brain,
it's like two rivers intersecting
on a vast basalt plain.

They merge at their angle
and pass right through
the way a ghost insults a wall.

Then they go on
in their old directions
toward the same legendary horizon.

Weightlifter

The weightlifter stares down at the bar
as he would stare at a corpse
to confirm its estrangement
and resolve the paradox of his hope and fear
that such a weight might rise in time on its own.

If the mind were a lever...
But it isn't.
And mass is sad. Every particle
mourns its lost state of just falling through space.
On the lip of sleep sometimes we have been
startled by a sudden drop,
the memory of that time.

No wonder then
the simple drama of his heft
draws us like fire.

When he empties his lungs like a bellows
to make room for the air that will be his groan
we quicken in our own heaviness,
convinced in that instant
it's an element of light.

EKG

The finale to the physical his plant required.
Naked to the waist. Pants rolled up to the knee.
Betty, the bored RN, prepping the machinery.
"Lie back on the table, please."

He lies, and not so idly inquires
"What can this gadget tell you about my heart?"
She scowls (her work is not stimulating), replies
"The electric potential," her voice a dull text.

"We need it for your history." She oils the appointed flesh
with a lotion so frigid his nipples
jigger into kernels.
"What's that for? A point of contact? For conductivity?"

He takes her silence for a technical assent.
She attaches the leads to his legs, his chest.
"Don't talk now," she says,
"It screws up the reading."

Mute but unquiet he stares at the ceiling
while ink leaps saw-toothed across a chart

forging the signature of a heart whose whole
desire for the moment is to be writ

as one of the unremarkable hearts
of Betty's days and days.

Ma Petite Poeme Française

"oh my Cadette
do not neglect
the fall

or else
you'll never be
accepted by
the Universite
de Bonaire
where

by grace and gravity
you might arrive
at your full potential and be
awarded a degree
in terminal velocity
to proudly hang

in medias res
on the slipstream of
your absent face
certifying you were
once there
and fully aware
of that and this
and this and that"

Bells

distant heartless sons
return for my dying
still my sons, always my sons

Surrealist's Last Wishes

"Of course there can be no formal will.
Nevertheless, please burn my umbrella.
The rest goes naturally to my current amanuensis,
this bag the doctors kindly sewed to my side
since I am no longer lord of my bowels.

In the end, dear children, we all turn nature poet.
Our estimable dreams betray us with the ease
of light-fingered whores slipping out into the hall.

Please let this be my last facility.
There's more mercy in a hammer.
A hammer's wife, anyway."

Piano Teacher

Her parlor, sepulchral.
Cool, even August noon.

No one in it at the moment
to return her late

husband's (photo on the piano)
formal stare,

or hear
the wishful ticking of

the faux Louis Quinze
timepiece on the mantel,

smooth
the rumpled needle-point

antimacassar atop
the raspberry-colored

wing-chair, or choose
from among the thirteen

snow-globe paperweights
on the oval

walnut table
a favorite,

or declare
how the wax fruit on the étagère

looks real enough to eat,
or translate

the mindless clucking
over the lace-

curtained window-seat
(from the wind-chime made

of cowrie shells
animated just now

by a little breeze)
into human feeling.

Young Woman Juggles Oranges

Her eyes
address each orange
at the point

through which all pass
their highest height
where each a stunned

instant in the air demurs
as if expecting some
revelation,

another world
before descending once again
into the care of her hands,

the catch below
like earth accepting
every sorrow as a seed—

just so,
she encourages in three oranges
the dream of flight.

One drops.
She curses, sighs, stoops
to pick it up

and begin again.
But first she must gather herself,
keeping perfectly still,

not a breath until
those merciless predators pass:
her *sadness* and her *hope*

that all this dropping
may one day blossom
and her hands

be transfigured into verse,
and the earth itself
dissolve around its harvest

leaving just pulse, buoyancy.
Charm.
Glow.

1912. Polar Explorer Addresses His Betrothed

"Dear Girl, forgive
this miserable scrawl,
issue of the cold's economy.
Believe me, I would write
a whole world but cannot
keep my hand long
outside the mitten.

How I miss our nights, my soul!
There is none at this latitude to deny
the blank plain going on
all white in every direction.
What wouldn't I give
for some little darkness
other than my own.

Darling, some nasty frost
has pilfered three of my toes,
but you mustn't mourn
what I scarcely miss.
Fiddlesticks, I say!
But now I know why we sleep in the dogs
and dream only dog dreams.
Cynicism is essential here.
My breath turns to ice right in my beard.

And poor Captain!
He no longer speaks
but growls like a beast.
His lips have gone black
and it hurts him to make words.
We still must be pretty far from our achievement.

I took the readings yesterday.
Captain had no feeling in his thumbs.
The horizon is God's mouth, open.
I made this remark and Captain smiled
causing himself such pain
tears poured from his eyes

freezing immediately on his cheeks
like tiny glaciers.
Poor Captain!
We must keep going he insists
just to stay where we are.
Just to remain men.

See?
This page does not ask to be filled
yet these words keep marching across the emptiness of it
just like our expedition heaving itself over the snow!
So onward, I say,
to the true pole,
that point from which every direction is the same.
How I long for it!
Because until I have stood there, Love,
I cannot return with all my heart
to you."

Hero Redux

He left
historically invisible
in the latest cuts
just a hint of blue
like a future nation
tall enough to shadow our provisions
thin enough to slip himself
under the locked door of the future

But now he's back
a mulching clod
gone native in the truest sense
wearing his roots like a hat

Uh oh.

Now we'll have to
adopt his map
as if it were
a painful scar
lift a glass of cheer
to his glassy stare
kiss his snakebites
and concur with his theory
that the horizon is hungry
and hinged like a jaw

Uh oh.

We'll have to turn his name
into an adjective
his flag into the wind
applaud him wildly
when he laps our mirrors
having traded his spoon
for a mood

And what happens when he remembers
we promised him our children
if he came back with a world
in which we could survive without him?

Shelf Life

Goodness has limits.
Blurred ink cites the last salutary date
after which you take your chances.
Yesterday's crimson giblets
fade to an ominous gray.

We survive suspecting life.
If something grows on something call it spoiled,
throw it away.
Unregenerate genesis is the bane of civilization.
Only periodic holocaust

can certify the store. Vichyssoise
from a faultless can killed
a family of five in Illinois.
Milk goes off.
Goodness expires.

In heaven
they boil everything.
The soul tastes neither bitter nor sweet.
Rice they found at pharaoh's feet
unmolested for millennia
is thought for food.

The dead eat light it seems.
The dead stay fit.

New Ghost

All this unfinished business and the avenue closed for despairs!
I kiss the concrete unrequitedly.
Smack! And again, *smack!*
I shrink to the full intent of nothingness
but the last O won't invert.
Puffed, I remain an O.

It's so much work, leaving the world!
I get stuck in some lawyer's cigar smoke,
in the comb of some remembered rain.
Stuck in a *faux pas* of neutrinos
and the aerial perjury of a favorite song.

Oh, inference!
No antiseptic can arrest you!
No death bleach you!
I'm ashamed I still have feelings.
I go back and forth through walls
trying to filter that stain.

Home

18 Cherry Street

Silence say the Masters
is the one bridge to the other world
where what's true
is truer than here.

Where I live
each tree has its quorum of grackles
that enjoins the many watchdogs to bark all day
at the succession of jet planes grousing over head
low in the critical approach.
Horns blare up and down my street
and doors slam—citizens getting out of their cars
to punch each other in the nose.

To make that crossing, find that bridge.
Find it or build it, the Masters say.

But here
the tradition between the last swallow and the ensuing psalm
is the bottle shattered on the curb.
A wealth of infants fills the air
with lung-loads of raw woe
over the drone of a hundred TV sets and the close
harmony of distant sirens and someone's libidinous cat.
The slightest breeze and my windows rattle.

I will never understand all I love.

Tell me, Masters
what shall I do residing on this shore
but praise every distraction?
For each one reminds me of nothing but itself,
and that's a kind of truth, isn't it?

Listen. Each time I shift my weight
this old wooden chair makes
a human sound.
The dogs are barking.
I'm here to tell you God loves noise.
Oyez! Oyez!

Metal Fatigue

An axle quits
spilling a quarter-mile of nectarines along the interstate.
She just went for no reason, insists the trucker to the trooper
who must file a report.

Another routine approach.
But passengers near the tail see the landing gear topple,
falling to land on its own.
The Captain croons the word *malfunction* like a lullaby, with finesse.
But travelers prefer abuse to misfortune,
Sabotage would be preferable.
Easier to accept.

A man wakes up suddenly in the middle of the night.
His dressing mirror has fallen to the floor,
shattered into a thousand slivers.
He suspects the supernatural.
It's safer to blame ghosts than to believe
a toggle-bolt made of U.S. steel might have secret human desires.

*

Don't you get tired sometimes?
Tired of mornings,
of washing your face, tending to your bowels?
Tired of pulling on your clothes,
of eating, of working, tired,
tired of the vertical life?
Don't you get tired? I do.

When the boiler explodes
I'm suddenly aware of our kinship.
When my key breaks off in the lock
how much better I understand it than before.
Who am I to pass judgement when a submarine gives in to the ocean
and refuses to rise? I,
who am alloyed likewise,

mind and flesh constantly debasing one another.
Shall I demand more from cast iron or aluminum
than from my foundering heart?

The mirror has fallen from the wall. Of course it has.
Someday I'll let go too and fall,
and sleep like ore invulnerable under a mountain.

But this cold particular morning
the radiator shudders and clanks.
When I turn it on the faucet moans and spits
as if it were dreaming again of the forge.
And weren't we cast also forcibly in a changing fire?
Don't we dream all night too and wake up exhausted?

The radiator shudders. I know how it feels.
Blessings on the pen that breaks in the middle of my name.
And bless the fillings that desert my teeth, exposing nerve.

Some Men Deliver a Store Window

Summer's riots,
the lootings and the fires,
have played themselves out—
not yet the jeweler's angina.
Braced in the open
doorway of his shop,
he watches two men
carry his order from their truck.

Their burden's invisible,
but ponderous apparently,
and delicate and treacherous
in the migrant autumn wind.
Uniform in blue gabardine
they move at a pallbearer's gait
heaving dark oaths
against their own necessary
tenderness as they mount the curb.

The jeweler chews his bottom lip,
can feel his pulse deep in his teeth.
His business will not end:

The eternal courtship of the eye.

He's replacing the plywood once again
with a vulnerable transparence,
trusting nothing but a poor heart
can ever ruin him.
Nothing but his own poor heart
riddled with desires.
Nothing.
Except maybe the wind
which the men carrying glass
lacerate with their curses
and which, without thinking,
the jeweler increases by heaving a sigh,
his breath scented with pickle and onion.

So Long

So long as the days themselves
carry on, promiscuous,
disappearing like water into water,
and at night

so long as the desolate stars
will profane their desolation
and bejewel our precious versions,
unremonstrant as we bead them into Lion,
Ladle, or Virgin—any tolerable sign—

a man can carve out a place for himself
among the things he doesn't notice,
or having noticed, turned away,
hoping that way
to make a virtue of Fate—

as when Don Juan, that great romancer,
arrived at some upscale occasion, entered
the buzzing hall to find, by a staggering chance,
all his lovers come together,
each one believing she
was first, best, or only
because he's let her think so,
none knowing of others,
but perhaps all knowing now.

What an elegant mess, the Truth!
Like being born again!

And remember, one has only to suffer to survive anything
so long as there are wiling days
and at night
great mute confections of stars.

To a Bombing Comic

What Christ-like passion keeps you on your feet?
The holy spasms you entreat lie limp
and heavy as braided dough in the stomachs of your audience.

Silence opens another vein.
Without a tourniquet soon
this sparse beer-soaked backroom
will bleed into infinite space.

It's too late now for practice in the mirror,
pulling your face through to the other side.
Too late to descend the slippery cadences of
that netherworld to reclaim your hysterical bride.

This world is real and hungry for your dying.
All anyone can hear is your words eating you.

Stand, then, in your dazzling crown of sweat
like any old god, unloved, alone,
until your words are done.

Vegas

All night
I have felt the suction of hope
from the slipstream of loss and losers
nibbling at the nape of my neck
like the strippers I used to pay
to make me feel like a man.

In this embrace of bad hands and ceiling mirrors,
surveillance cameras playing every angle,
I can feel something like the murmur of sex
licking its way slowly up my spine,
alerting me the next pot is mine.

Or the next.

Outside, the desert sky swirls with stars
playing their cosmic game of musical chairs
to a Jack-in-the-Box version
of *Pop Goes the Weasel.*

That's the way the money goes.

Somebody has to win.

Gabriel in the Warehouse

Just the tip of one wing
jutting out from behind a stack of drums and pallets,
barely brushing what's noticeable
and so subtly no one
could conceive it a wing.

Descend, he was told,
and be visible to good men
as a harbinger of life everlasting.

But nausea gripped him
as he crawled down the air-ducts,
so he's hedging awhile, hiding essentially,
obeying the letter, as the saying goes,
though hardly the spirit of his order
until his stomach can adjust
to the pressure of mortality.

Not like the old days,
astounding shepherds in the nibbled hills,
strutting through the willows into the eyes of virgins
as they bathed at twilight in the river,
brighter, they would breathlessly report,
than a hundred suns.

Here his aura is dispersed in the common wash of fluorescent tubes
that hum and spit above. And his eyes,
all silver, ache and water
as he squints through the crate-slats at the warehousemen
on their morning break,
heads bowed in silence over steaming coffees.

This is the moment, he knows,
devised on high for his heraldry.
He shifts his weight from one foot to the other
like a schoolchild gone blank at recitation.

From the far wall by the loading dock
the punch-clock stares straight at him,

each metallic click of it declaring
eternity has no business here.

Who will blame him then,
though we know it is his job,
if he does not step out amid the forklifts and the hoists
blowing his horn?
Who has not felt that gnawing at the bowels
like a feast of birds?

Any Bird

To the Iroquois, crows
from the north in the month
of crackling pines
were.

An eagle before the battle
spied by Caesar's *auspices*
heartened the cohorts more than steel.

And swallows meaning home,
bluebirds gladness,
and dove, the risen Christ.

There used to be a wealth of signs
before all the X's of our days gone by.

I teach my children with a backward eye
to notice markings bled and indistinct.

It's a gold finch. I think it is.
A purple sorrow. A swift.
A speckled thrush.

It's something, anyway.
Something fine.
Any bird these days is good luck.

The End

April. A waffling crackle. Then, thud. I run
to the back of our house and see the doddered oak we named
Woodpecker Hilton, far anchor to the clothesline since
before we moved in, toppled across the percolating lawn, broken
in equal sections like one of those columns excavated at Pompeii.
My wife's nightgown, our powder-blue sheets, my favorite flannel
        shirt, our
baby's tiny socks and well-washed onesies all thrust down into
        tangled throes
like the sudden victims the diggers found. The end has happened.
We knew it would. The weight pulled down the tree.
Surveying the mess, I'm not surprised nor dismayed—
except by my pleasure at the beauty.

The Impossible House

You might wake up in it.

If you do, look quick!
Before the windows have a chance
to join forces with the mirrors!

See?

Home is everywhere!

Fission

—Upon hearing the news of the pending divorce of two
friends long-married

You say the split was amicable.
I know that's just a line.

You were our perfect couple.
Everything seemed fine.

From the outside, graced with distance
And a weakness for harmony,

Ignoring nature's compliance
With corruptibility

(Everything in existence
Disintegrates eventually)

We didn't have a clue
What was undoing you.

*

Please tell me now what should I pray for?
To whom and for what give praise?

There's an endless stream of shysters at my door
Hawking cut-rate ends-of-days.

And all the old gods are gone,
Camera-shy, hiding from our most

Sensitive up-to-date theologies and telescopes,
Leaving us (I mean *me*) all alone

Wondering whether one
And one were ever

Really meant
To be together.

Don't Look Down

—*an homage to Wile E. Coyote of the old Warner Brother's Roadrunner cartoons*

Coyote.
Sensei.
Paradigm.

The more I've learned
From your technicolor mania
Than from all the monotonous beards
Of academia
Identifies me
Like a peculiar scar.

Epitome of desire.
Full-throttle.
Committed like an arrow
Hurtling through empty air
Toward the one thing
You really want—
Homer couldn't imagine
Such a hero,
For whom each failure
Blossoms like an Easter lily
To grace the world's ineptitudes.

An anvil for a head,
Or flattened by the real locomotive emerging
From the tunnel you contrived to paint
(A triumph of *trompe l'oeil*)
On the canyon wall.
Anxious to sell your soul
To the Devil of your own imagination,

Trusting if you don't look down
You'll never fall.

And if you do
The very obsession that wounds you
Will heal you.
And you'll rise from the powders of the desert floor
Splendid and whole as that mythical phoenix
Which, if you could snatch it from the ashes,
You wouldn't hesitate for one second to devour.

Drums

Dad, dead
His ashes spread

For a year Mom sighed
Then Mom died

We sold the house
Under market price

(Times being tough)
And all the stuff

Of all their years
Sifted among smiles and tears

We went through
As survivors do

To make peace
With warring memories

And soothe old rues and guilts
Beneath some tattered quilts

In a corner of the attic, hidden there
Behind boxes of vintage Tupperware

Its latent tempos unbidden
Since the summer of 1967

I found my old drum kit, a Ludwig
Still set up as if anxious for a gig

On the snare lay a set of sticks
Sporting some old rim-shot cicatrix

Surprised the relic still existed
Memory's protocols insisted

I sit down and play
My brother frowned and turned away

I was never very good
But at 16 I could

Keep the beat to *Hang*
On Sloopy, syncopate *Chain Gang*

The Sam Cooke song, kick ass
On *Looey-Looey* and *Jumpin' Jack Flash*

Work tom-tom and gong on *Back Door Man*
Good enough for a garage band

Playing venues like Knights of Columbus
And Jaycee mixers. Three of us

Calling ourselves
Satan's Horny Little Elves

With a play-list of maybe twenty covers
Fast for hip-shakers, slow for lovers

We built a town-wide reputation
Famous the duration

Of two sultry summers. Then we split
For college and that was it

That was it for a lot
Of stuff I've since forgot

Let slip into the vast
Uninventoried storehouse of the past

My first girlfriend was a second-generation Greek
(Graced with Athena's brow and Aphrodite's cheek)

Harriet, a classmate's moody sister
My knees spazzed out when I first kissed her

I loved her in my prodigious way
Not much truth to give but lots of words to say

Although my heart was reeling
I was so frightened of the feeling

I could never express it honestly
I was the subtle prince of probity

None of us back then
Could imagine an end

To anything, so high were we
On the dope of possibility

We approached each day
Like an all-you-can-eat buffet

Believing appetite alone would pay dividends
So I went on to college and other girlfriends

Letting the embers of my first genuine passion
Die from lack of attention

And my commitment to the drum
Prove just an adolescent enthusiasm

Later I heard a rumor Harriet had married
Young and pregnant, miscarried

Twice, divorced the guy (a troubled Green Beret)
Who one year later (to the day)

Leapt from a window (twelve stories)
Impaling himself amid morning glories

That twined around the wrought-iron fence
Below. What unkind condolence

To offer to taste her bitter tears
Now after thirty-five years

So long since we conversed
Any sympathy just lip-service at its worst

When we were together I gave what love I could
Puny, self-referent, not much good

To a creature steeped in feeling
As she was. Without stealing

How could I give you my heart, Harriet?
I didn't own it yet

I hope you're well-loved now. Did you re-marry?
I've thought of you but rarely

Since our high-school days
Would you blossom in my gaze

Should we meet again or not bother?
Would we even recognize each other?

And why now staring down at
The random dings in my old hi-hat

Have I conjured the dark allure of your eyes
And suddenly want to apologize

For all I did and didn't do?
Your destiny wooed you

Mine ruled otherwise. Sticks in hand
Now I'm poised to count-in the band

Instead I hear the quiet say
"Please let me stay this way"

Since my brother and sister went
Downstairs to survey the basement

The attic reconciled with silence like a tomb
(The way at night a flower folds up its bloom)

All I can hear is my heart keeping time
Faithful iambs marching toward a final rhyme

Let that old rhythm in this new emptiness be the way
I honor the drums I used to play.

Number Theory

Nine in the first place means trouble at the gate.
Three can have no consequence beyond the third condition.
Eight is like the anus of an infinite appetite.
In four's place, five cannot remember its own prediction.

Six, at the eleventh hour, succumbs to deep psychosis.
Eleven escapes inherently on the wings of a mirror.
A cough from the tomb where zero lies
means it's safe to believe anything you hear.

Seven, in its own place, weeps to heal—like a wounded tree.
In any other place it cures like salt.
Ten paces back and forth, back and forth—a neurotic sentry
starved for sleep, ordering shadows to halt,

Two defines herself with the smug confidence of a sum.
Every morning, one wakes up alone in a different room.

Acknowledgments

Grateful acknowledgment is made to the following publications in which some of these poems first appeared.

American Poetry Review: "Gabriel in the Warehouse," "18 Cherry Street," "Humiliation," "Metal Fatigue," "So Long," and "Snow, Christmas Morning," which previously appeared as "December"

Grand Street: "Halftime," "Number Theory"

The Paris Review: "Nocturne with Cows"

Ploughshares: "Ice Storm," "Coeymans," "Calling"

photo by Dion Ogust

Adam LeFevre was born in Albany, New York in 1950, and raised in Coeymans, an old Dutch hamlet on the west bank of the Hudson River. He studied at Albany Academy, Williams College, and the University of Iowa. After a stint of itinerant labor across the country he settled in New York City and began a career as an actor, on and off Broadway, in television and film. His previous collections of poetry are *Everything All At Once,* from Wesleyan University Press, and *Ghost Light,* a chapbook from Finishing Line Press. His plays have been produced in New York City and regionally. He is the father of two grown children, Tate, an anthropology professor at Franklin and Marshall College, and Isaac, a film-maker.

He currently resides in New Paltz, New York.

The Green Rose Prize

2014:   Kathleen Halme
           My Multiverse

2013:   Ralph Angel
           Your Moon

2012:   Jaswinder Bolina
           Phantom Camera

2011:   Corey Marks
           The Radio Tree

2010:   Seth Abramson
           Northerners

2009:   Malinda Markham
           Having Cut the Sparrow's Heart

2008:   Patty Seyburn
           Hilarity

2007:   Jon Pineda
           The Translator's Diary

2006:   Noah Eli Gordon
           A Fiddle Pulled from the Throat of a Sparrow

2005:   Joan Houlihan
           The Mending Worm

2004:   Hugh Seidman
           Somebody Stand Up and Sing

2003:   Christine Hume
           Alaskaphrenia
           Gretchen Mattox
           Buddha Box

2002:   Christopher Bursk
           Ovid at Fifteen